The Science of Attraction

Pasindu A

Published by Creative2Hemispheres, 2024.

While every precaution has been taken in the preparation of this book, the publisher assumes no responsibility for errors or omissions, or for damages resulting from the use of the information contained herein.

THE SCIENCE OF ATTRACTION

First edition. March 8, 2024.

ISBN: 979-8224121540

Written by Pasindu A.

Also by Pasindu A

Find the Man of Your Dreams: 10 Traits of High-Value Men
Miles Apart Hearts Together: 10 Ways to Thrive in a Long Distance Relationship
Financial Planning for the Modern Couple: 10 Ways to Manage Your Finances in Today's Economy
The Disaster Preparedness Survival Guide: 10 Tips on How to Plan and Prepare for Any Emergency
The Secret to a Great Sex Life
The Science of Attraction

Watch for more at https://healthfactsbydoctorpasindu.com/.

Table of Contents

To all my readers who encourage me to write!

The Science of Attraction

PASINDU A

Foreword

———

Beyond butterflies and stolen glances: Dive into captivating science of attraction!

Ever wondered why you're drawn to one person but not another? Why does a fleeting gaze ignite a spark, while hours of conversation leave you cold? **"The Science of Attraction"** peels back the curtain on the captivating mystery of human desire, revealing the biological, psychological, and even cultural forces that orchestrate the symphony of attraction.

This isn't your typical self-help guide or shallow rom-com. **This is a deep dive into the very essence of what makes us fall, stay, and drift apart.** It's a scientific detective story where wit meets wisdom, and every chapter unveils a new clue:

- **Unmask the allure of physical features**: Discover the evolutionary whispers hidden in symmetry, the seductive power of scent, and how cultural norms paint beauty in a thousand vibrant hues.
- **Delve into the depths of the mind**: Explore the charm of wit, the allure of shared values, and the intoxicating pull of a kindred spirit. Understand how personality, intelligence, and humor play their part in the grand play of attraction.
- **Experience the emotional rollercoaster**: Witness how vulnerability ignites intimacy, shared laughter sparks joy, and passion paints emotions in fiery hues. Learn how emotional connection deepens attraction and shapes lasting bonds.
- **Go beyond the individual**: Discover how social factors like

status and popularity cast their fleeting shadows on desire. Travel across continents to see how cultural expectations influence mating preferences and ignite unique passions.

- **Peek into the future:** Contemplate the possibilities of AI-powered matchmaking and the ethical quandaries of genetic manipulation. Imagine a world where virtual connections blur the lines between reality and fantasy, forever altering the way we navigate the realm of attraction.

"The Science of Attraction" is more than just a book; it's an invitation. It's an invitation to shed preconceived notions and embrace the beautiful complexity of desire. It's an invitation to understand yourself, your unique patterns of attraction, and the intricate connections that bind you to others. It's a chance to rewrite your own love story, armed with the knowledge of science and the wisdom of self-discovery.

So, are you ready to unlock the secrets of desire? Turn the page, dear reader, and let the captivating dance of attraction begin.

Remember, this book is not just for the romantics; it's for anyone curious about the human experience, anyone who has ever wondered why the heart beats faster for some and remains silent for others. It's a journey of self-discovery, a quest for understanding, and a celebration of the beautiful tapestry of human connection.

Join the scientific exploration of attraction today!

Introduction: Unlocking the Secrets of Desire: A Journey into the Science of Attraction

———

What makes us fall for someone? Is it a fleeting spark ignited by a captivating glance, or a slow burn fueled by shared laughter and whispered secrets? Is it the chiseled jawline and sculpted physique, or the mischievous glint in their eyes and the wisdom in their words?

The truth is, attraction is a symphony, an intricate dance where biology, psychology, and environment all join hands, weaving a tapestry of desire as unique as each beating heart.

In "The Science of Attraction," we embark on a captivating journey into the very heart of this mesmerizing phenomenon. We will dissect the alluring power of physical features, from the symmetry that whispers of genetic health to the scent that evokes unspoken promises. We'll delve into the labyrinth of the mind, unraveling the charm of wit, the allure of shared values, and the intoxicating pull of a kindred spirit. We'll explore the depths of emotion, where vulnerability ignites intimacy and shared laughter sparks joy, forging bonds that transcend the ephemeral.

But our exploration doesn't stop at the individual. We'll step outside to the bustling social stage, where whispers of status and popularity cast their fleeting shadows on desire. We'll travel across continents, discovering how cultural norms paint beauty in a thousand vibrant hues, shaping preferences and igniting passions unique to each corner of the world.

This isn't just a journey into the science of attraction; it's a quest for self-discovery. We'll unlock the evolutionary whispers embedded in our genes, the primal urges that guide our choices and sculpt our desires. We'll peek into the intricate dance of neurons and hormones, witnessing the biological fireworks that erupt with a stolen glance or a whispered word.

And yes, we'll turn our gaze to the future, where technology reshapes the landscape of love and desire. We'll contemplate the possibilities of AI-powered matchmaking and the ethical quandaries of genetic manipulation. We'll imagine a world where virtual connections blur the lines between reality and fantasy, forever altering the way we navigate the intoxicating realm of attraction.

"The Science of Attraction" is more than just a book; it's an invitation. It's an invitation to shed preconceived notions and embrace the beautiful complexity of desire. It's an invitation to explore the fascinating interplay of biology, psychology, and environment that orchestrates the symphony of attraction. It's an invitation to understand ourselves, our desires, and the intricate connections that bind us to others.

So, are you ready to unlock the secrets of desire? Are you ready to embark on a journey that will forever change the way you look at love, at connection, and at yourself? Turn the page, dear reader, and let the dance begin!

Chapter 1. Understanding the Science of Physical Attraction: Beyond the "Beauty Standard"

————

While physical features play a role in initial attraction, it's important to remember that beauty is subjective and multifaceted. Here's a dive into the science behind physical attraction, focusing on aspects both men and women can work on to enhance their overall attractiveness:

Embrace the Power of Perception:

- **Symmetry:** Studies suggest we find symmetrical faces more attractive, possibly due to their perceived association with good health and genetic fitness. However, what constitutes "symmetry" can vary culturally, so embrace your unique features and focus on highlighting your natural balance.
- **Facial Features:** Certain features, like clear skin, bright eyes, and a full smile, might be universally attractive due to their association with health and friendliness. Remember, though, that confidence and emotional expressiveness play a major role in how your features are perceived.
- **Body Type:** Cultural ideals for body types shift over time and across geographical regions. Instead of chasing impossible standards, focus on maintaining a healthy lifestyle and building a physique that makes you feel strong and confident. This inner confidence will shine through and be more attractive than any specific body shape.

Scent of Attraction:

Our sense of smell is surprisingly powerful when it comes to attraction. Pheromones, natural chemical signals, play a subtle role in influencing our subconscious perceptions of others. However, personal hygiene and a pleasant, fresh scent are far more important factors in creating a positive olfactory impression.

Beyond the Physical:

Remember, physical attraction is just one factor in the complex recipe of overall attractiveness. Here are some other aspects both men and women can work on to make a lasting impression:

- **Confidence and Positivity:** People who exude confidence and optimism are naturally more attractive. Focus on cultivating self-worth and radiating positive energy through your body language and interactions.
- **Communication Skills:** Being able to communicate effectively and engagingly makes you more interesting and attractive. Actively listen, express yourself clearly, and show genuine interest in others.
- **Humor and Playfulness:** Sharing a laugh and having fun together is a powerful bonding experience. Develop your sense of humor and don't be afraid to show your playful side.
- **Passion and Purpose:** People who are passionate about their interests and have a sense of purpose in life are magnetic. Pursue your passions, contribute to your community, and live with purpose to radiate an aura of authenticity and fulfillment.

Ultimately, while physical features can play a role in initial attraction, true beauty and allure go far beyond the surface. By focusing on these additional aspects, both men and women can cultivate an attractive personality and become genuinely captivating individuals who draw others in with their confidence, warmth, and inner spark.

Remember: It's important to appreciate your unique characteristics and celebrate your individual beauty. Embrace what makes you special and focus on becoming the best version of yourself, inside and out. That's the most attractive quality anyone can possess.

Enhancing Your Inner and Outer Glow: A Guide to Feeling Confident and Attractive

True beauty shines from both within and without. It's about embracing your individual features, cultivating a healthy lifestyle, and radiating positive energy. While physical appearance plays a role in initial attraction, the key to real magnetism lies in a holistic approach that focuses on well-being, confidence, and personal style.

Embrace Your Uniqueness:

Instead of chasing impossible beauty standards, celebrate what makes you special. Your unique features, quirks, and passions are what set you apart and contribute to your personal charm. Focus on enhancing your natural beauty by:

- **Taking care of your skin:** A consistent skincare routine with cleansing, moisturizing, and sun protection can work wonders.
- **Maintaining good oral hygiene:** A bright smile is universally attractive. Brush and floss regularly, and consider professional teeth whitening for an extra boost.
- **Getting enough sleep:** Sleep deprivation shows on your face and affects your energy levels. Aim for 7-8 hours of restful sleep each night.
- **Eating a balanced diet:** Nourishing your body with healthy foods reflects in your skin, hair, and overall well-being. Choose plenty of fruits, vegetables, and whole grains.
- **Exercising regularly:** Physical activity not only improves your

physical health but also boosts your mood and confidence. Find activities you enjoy, whether it's dancing, swimming, or hitting the gym.

Present Yourself with Confidence:

Confidence is the ultimate accessory. When you feel good about yourself, it shows in your posture, your smile, and the way you interact with others. Here are some tips to cultivate confidence:

- **Wear clothes that fit you well and make you feel good:** It's not about following trends blindly, but choosing clothes that flatter your body type and reflect your personal style.
- **Maintain good posture:** Stand tall, shoulders back, and avoid slouching. Good posture makes you look and feel more confident.
- **Practice positive self-talk:** Challenge negative thoughts with affirmations and focus on your strengths and accomplishments.
- **Develop your social skills:** Make eye contact, smile genuinely, and be an active listener in conversations.

Scentual Allure:

A pleasant scent can leave a lasting positive impression. Here are some tips for personal fragrance:

- **Choose a scent that complements your personality:** Pick light, fresh scents for daytime and warmer, sensual aromas for evening.
- **Apply fragrance to pulse points:** Wrists, elbows, and behind the ears are good spots where the scent can waft up subtly.
- **Avoid overdoing it:** A few lightly applied spritzes are enough. You don't want to overpower anyone with your fragrance.

Beyond the Surface:

Remember, physical beauty is just one piece of the puzzle. True attractiveness comes from the inside out. Cultivate these qualities to enhance your inner glow:

- **Be kind and compassionate:** Kindness is a universally attractive quality. Treat others with respect and empathy.
- **Be passionate and curious:** Having interests and pursuing your passions makes you interesting and engaging.
- **Develop a sense of humor:** Laughter is a great way to connect with others and make a positive impression.
- **Be a good listener:** Show genuine interest in what others have to say and ask thoughtful questions.

Ultimately, the best way to be attractive is to be yourself. Embrace your unique qualities, cultivate your inner well-being, and radiate confidence. When you feel good about yourself, it shows, and you'll naturally attract people who appreciate you for who you are.

Additional Tips:

- Experiment with different hairstyles and makeup looks to find what flatters you best.
- Accessorize wisely to add a touch of personality to your outfits.
- Take care of your mental health: Stress and anxiety can show on your face. Practice relaxation techniques and seek professional help if needed.
- Develop a positive outlook on life: People who are optimistic and upbeat are naturally more attractive.

Remember, the journey to self-improvement is ongoing. Focus on making healthy choices, developing your inner qualities, and embracing your unique beauty. When you radiate confidence and positivity, you'll naturally draw people in, making you attractive to others in the most authentic and genuine way.

Chapter 2. The Magnetic Mind: Unraveling the Psychology of Attraction

―――

While physical beauty may spark initial interest, it's the unseen depths of psychology that truly ignite and sustain attraction. Beyond the facade of features lies a complex tapestry of personality traits, cognitive abilities, values, and shared experiences that draw us to specific individuals.

Let's delve into the fascinating world of psychological attraction, exploring the research-backed factors that make hearts beat a little faster.

Personality Parade: The Allure of Traits

Certain personality traits consistently emerge as magnets for attraction. Studies suggest we're drawn to individuals who possess:

- **Openness to Experience:** Open-minded individuals, curious about new things and adaptable to change, are perceived as intellectually stimulating and exciting partners. Research by Fehr et al. (2002) found greater openness correlated with higher desirability in online dating profiles.
- **Agreeableness:** Kindness, cooperativeness, and empathy make individuals enjoyable to be around, fostering feelings of warmth and safety. A study by Dion et al. (1972) showed people preferred others with agreeable personalities for long-term relationships.
- **Conscientiousness:** Reliable, organized, and goal-oriented individuals are perceived as responsible and dependable, qualities valued in potential partners. Research also found that conscientiousness positively correlated with perceived

attractiveness.

- **Emotional Stability:** Stable individuals, who manage their emotions effectively and avoid excessive negativity, create a sense of emotional security and calm. Research by Brown and Kring (2014) suggests emotional stability plays a crucial role in romantic partner selection.

Beyond these core traits, humor also emerges as a powerful attractor. A study by Miller (2000) revealed individuals who could make others laugh were perceived as more attractive and desirable. Humor not only signals intelligence and social skills but also creates positive emotions and fosters connection.

Intellectual Alchemy: The Spark of Minds

Intelligence, though not always explicitly stated, plays a subtle yet significant role in attraction. Studies by Fehr et al. (2002) and Luo et al. (2017) show individuals perceive higher intelligence as attractive, particularly in potential long-term partners. This may be due to its association with problem-solving abilities, adaptability, and stimulating conversation.

However, the type of intelligence that matters seems multifaceted. Moreover, research suggests emotional intelligence, the ability to understand and manage one's own emotions as well as those of others, is particularly valued in intimate relationships.

Shared Values: The Compass of Compatibility

Shared values serve as the compass guiding us towards compatible partners. We're naturally drawn to individuals who share our beliefs about important life aspects such as family, career, religion, and social responsibility. Studies by Sprecher et al. (1994) confirm the powerful role of value congruence in relationship satisfaction and stability.

Shared values go beyond mere agreement. It's about understanding and respecting each other's perspectives, even when they differ slightly. This creates a sense of mutual support, understanding, and long-term compatibility.

The Mirror Effect: Similarities that Attract

Research by Byrne and Clore (1973) introduced the "mere exposure effect," suggesting we tend to like things we're familiar with. This extends to interpersonal attraction, where we're drawn to individuals who share similarities with us. Studies found that individuals are more attracted to those who resemble them in physical appearance, personality traits, and even mannerisms.

This "mirror effect" could be partially explained by the ease of communication and comfort that arises from shared experiences and perspectives. However, it's important to note that excessive similarity can stifle personal growth and lead to a dull relationship.

The Rhythm of Reciprocity: Liking Those Who Like Us

The old adage "you get what you give" holds true in attraction as well. We're naturally drawn to individuals who express interest and liking towards us. This is explained by the principle of reciprocity, where we feel obligated to reciprocate positive feelings directed towards us. Studies by Berscheid et al. (1973) support this phenomenon, demonstrating that perceived liking increases our own attraction towards another person.

However, it's crucial to strike a balance between genuine interest and manipulative flattery. Excessively showering someone with undeserved compliments can backfire, creating the impression of insincerity or ulterior motives.

Unraveling the Attraction Cocktail:

It's important to remember that psychological attraction is rarely the result of a single factor. Instead, it's a complex blend of personality traits, intellectual compatibility, shared values, similarities, and perceived liking, all swirling together to create a potent cocktail of attraction.

Here are some additional insights:

Beyond the Obvious:

Research reveals that not all personality traits are equally attractive in all contexts. For example, a study by Buss and Barnes (1986) found men valued ambition and independence in potential short-term partners, while prioritizing kindness and warmth in long-term partners. Similarly, the perceived importance of intelligence can vary based on individual preferences and cultural expectations.

The Allure of Mystery:

While familiarity breeds attraction, a touch of mystery can also be captivating. Studies by Aron and Dion (1972) suggest that revealing oneself gradually, fostering an element of discovery, can keep the spark alive and prolong attraction. This doesn't imply being enigmatic or secretive, but rather strategically revealing certain aspects of yourself over time, letting the other person unravel your layers like an intriguing puzzle.

Breaking the Mold:

While the factors discussed above provide a broad understanding of psychological attraction, it's important to remember that individual preferences and lived experiences play a significant role.

Not everyone is drawn to the same set of traits or values. Some might prioritize spontaneity and excitement over stability, while others might find artistic temperament more attractive than conventional success. The beauty of attraction lies in its inherent diversity and individuality.

The Evolving Landscape:

The digital age has significantly altered the landscape of attraction. Online dating platforms, with their algorithms and filters, have streamlined the initial search for potential partners based on certain criteria. While this offers convenience and efficiency, it can also lead to overlooking individuals who don't neatly fit predefined categories. Remember, true attraction often goes beyond the metrics displayed on a screen, and genuine connection can blossom with someone who might not tick all the boxes on a virtual checklist.

Cultivating Your Attractant:

Understanding the psychology of attraction isn't about manipulating personalities or crafting a facade to attract others. It's about nurturing genuine self-growth and developing qualities that naturally exude charm and magnetism.

Invest in your well-being, explore your passions, cultivate your strengths, and radiate kindness and authenticity. When you are truly comfortable and confident in your own skin, it becomes a powerful attractor, drawing in individuals who appreciate you for who you are.

Ultimately, while psychological factors play a crucial role in attraction, it's important to remember that it's just one facet of a multifaceted experience.

Attraction is a dance of both the mind and the heart, a unique blend of chemistry, shared experiences, and the intangible sparks that ignite between two souls. By understanding the science and embracing your own individuality, you can navigate the intricate world of attraction with confidence and open your heart to meaningful connections.

Chapter 3. The Heartbeat of Connection: Unveiling the Power of Emotional Attraction

While physical allure and intellectual compatibility draw us in, it's the vibrant dance of emotions that truly deepens attraction and forges strong bonds. Beyond the initial flutter of desire lies a captivating symphony of intimacy, attachment, and passion, weaving threads of connection that bind us to another. Let's embark on a journey into the realm of emotional attraction, exploring the research-backed roles these vital emotions play in solidifying our relationships.

Intimacy: Unveiling the Soul:

Intimacy signifies the safe haven where we shed our masks and reveal our vulnerability, sharing our deepest thoughts, fears, and dreams. Studies by Reis and Patrick (1996) highlight the significance of intimacy in fostering feelings of closeness and emotional security. It's the glue that binds us, creating a space of unreserved acceptance and understanding.

This vulnerability isn't about spilling secrets or oversharing; it's about creating a comfortable environment for mutual openness. Research by Brown (2007) on vulnerability's power suggests that openly expressing our authentic selves, both our strengths and imperfections, is crucial for building genuine connection.

Attachment: Weaving Threads of Security:

Attachment, though often associated with childhood experiences, extends into adult relationships, providing a sense of security and emotional support. Studies by Bowlby (1982) and Hazan and Shaver

(1987) identify different attachment styles, ranging from secure, where partners feel comfortable relying on each other, to insecure, where anxiety or withdrawal characterize the bond.

Secure attachment provides the bedrock for a healthy relationship. We know our partner is there for us, offering a safe haven in times of need and celebrating our triumphs. This sense of security, highlights, fosters emotional well-being and strengthens the bond.

Passion: The Embers of Desire:

Passion adds a spark of excitement and vibrancy to the relationship. It's the intoxicating mix of physical attraction, emotional intensity, and shared enthusiasm. Studies by Hatfield and Sprecher (1986) differentiate passionate love from companionate love, emphasizing the role of intense emotions and physiological arousal in the former.

While the initial intensity of passion might wane over time, it can be nurtured through shared experiences, expressions of affection, and maintaining a sense of playfulness. Research suggests that actively engaging in romantic behaviors keeps the flame of passion alive and contributes to overall relationship satisfaction.

The Emotional Cocktail: Synergy in the Mix:

It's important to remember that these emotions don't exist in isolation. They blend and intertwine, creating a unique tapestry of connection. Intimacy fosters deeper attachment, while secure attachment allows passion to flourish. Similarly, the embers of passion can keep intimacy fresh and prevent attachment from becoming stagnant. Research supports this holistic approach, suggesting that a combination of positive emotions, including intimacy, passion, and commitment, contributes to relationship satisfaction and longevity.

From Spark to Flame: How Emotional Connection Deepens Attraction:

Emotional connection acts as the fertile ground where attraction blossoms into something deeper. As intimacy builds, we see beyond the surface, appreciating the intricate beauty of our partner's inner world. This deeper understanding fuels attraction, making us yearn for their presence and cherish their vulnerabilities.

Secure attachment strengthens this bond, providing a bedrock of comfort and support. Knowing we can rely on our partner through challenges and share moments of joy amplifies the feeling of safety and connection, enhancing our attraction.

The embers of passion, when nurtured and sustained, keep the relationship vibrant and engaging. Shared laughter, playful banter, and expressions of tenderness remind us of the electrifying connection that drew us together in the first place.

Beyond the Research: Cultivating Emotional Connection:

Understanding the nuances of emotional attraction is beneficial, but fostering these emotions in your own relationship requires active effort. Here are some ways to cultivate a deeper emotional connection:

- **Practice active listening:** Truly hear your partner without distractions, giving them your full attention and validating their feelings.
- **Share openly and honestly:** Express your thoughts, fears, and vulnerabilities in a safe space, building trust and intimacy.
- **Be present in the moment:** Put away distractions and engage fully in shared activities, fostering connection and creating lasting memories.
- **Express your affection regularly:** Words and gestures of love,

both big and small, keep the flame of passion alive and remind your partner of your feelings.

- **Offer support and encouragement:** Be your partner's rock, their safe haven during challenges, and their cheerleader in their pursuits.

Remember, Every Love Story is Different:

While common threads weave through the tapestry of emotional attraction, it's crucial to remember that every relationship is unique. The specific blend of emotions and experiences that resonate most profoundly will differ from couple to couple. Some might thrive on the whirlwind intensity of passionate love, while others find solace in the quietude of companionship and deep understanding. The key lies in appreciating your partner's emotional needs and tailoring your connection to cater to them.

Breaking Down Barriers: Vulnerability and Growth:

Cultivating emotional connection can be challenging. Our past experiences, anxieties, and communication styles can create roadblocks to intimacy and vulnerability. It's okay to navigate these challenges, acknowledging past scars and working together to overcome them. Seek professional help if needed, remember that communication is key, and celebrate each step towards greater emotional openness.

Beyond the Honeymoon: Nurturing the Flame:

Emotional connection, like a garden, needs tending. Even the strongest bonds require effort to thrive. Regular communication, shared experiences, and expressing gratitude are essential nutrients for a fulfilling relationship. Don't take each other for granted, constantly strive to learn more about each other, and embrace the journey of growth together.

Embracing the Symphony of Emotions:

The heart of a thriving relationship beats to the rhythm of countless emotions. Joy, sorrow, anger, and everything in between contribute to the rich tapestry of connection. Learn to navigate these emotions together, offering support and understanding during difficult times and amplifying the joy of shared triumphs.

Emotional attraction is not a static state; it's a dynamic ebb and flow of feelings that evolves over time. By understanding the intricate interplay of emotions and nurturing the delicate threads of connection, we can create relationships that are not just passionate, but also deeply meaningful and enduring.

Remember, the secret to unlocking the true power of attraction lies not in seeking perfection, but in embracing the beautiful symphony of emotions that bind us to another soul.

Chapter 4. Navigating the Labyrinth: How Social Factors Shape Attraction

Beyond the fluttering of hearts and the meeting of minds, the intricate dance of attraction unfolds in the vibrant tapestry of social life. From the allure of popularity to the subtle whisper of social status, the dynamics of our social standing exert a powerful influence on whom we find attractive. Let's journey into this fascinating realm, exploring the research-backed roles of social factors and how they can enhance or diminish our attraction to others.

The Spotlight Effect: Basking in the Glow of Popularity:

Research by Dion et al. (1972) introduced the concept, "halo effect" demonstrating that individuals perceive attractive people as more popular, and vice versa. This phenomenon, highlights the tendency to attribute positive qualities to those deemed popular by others. Studies by Berscheid et al. (1973) further support this notion, suggesting that the perception of popularity can enhance an individual's attractiveness, even if their inherent physical features remain unchanged.

So, why does popularity hold such sway in the realms of attraction? It could be explained by the association between popularity and positive social cues. Individuals perceived as popular are often seen as confident, sociable, and well-adjusted, qualities traditionally viewed as attractive. Additionally, the validation offered by being part of someone else's popularity halo can enhance our self-esteem, making us feel more attractive ourselves.

Social Status: The Ladder of Desirability:

Social status, intertwined with financial success, professional achievements, and social power, also plays a significant role in attraction. Studies reveal that individuals of higher social status are perceived as more attractive, particularly in short-term mating contexts. This tendency may have evolved from an ancestral link between social status and access to resources, making a high-status partner advantageous for offspring survival.

However, the influence of social status can be complex and context-dependent. Research suggests that the allure of high social status diminishes in long-term relationship settings, where compatibility and shared values hold greater weight. Additionally, societal perceptions of "high status" can evolve over time and across cultures, challenging the universality of this factor's influence.

Group Affiliation: Finding Connection in Shared Colors:

Our affiliation with specific social groups, be it based on cultural background, hobbies, or professional circles, can also influence our attraction patterns.

Studies by Fiske (1993) suggest that we tend to find individuals from our own groups more attractive, a phenomenon known as "in-group bias." This preference may arise from the comfort and familiarity found within shared identity markers, fostering a sense of trust and potential compatibility.

However, in-group bias can also pose limitations. An overreliance on shared group affiliation can restrict our social circle and diminish the possibility of forming meaningful connections with individuals from different backgrounds. The key lies in striking a balance between appreciating the comfort of shared identity while remaining open to the enriching potential of diversity.

Enhancing Attraction: Social Factors as Tools, Not Masters:

Understanding the influence of social factors on attraction does not necessitate succumbing to their sway. Recognizing their role can empower us to make conscious choices and navigate the social landscape with greater clarity. Here are some ways to utilize social factors to enhance attraction:

- **Cultivating confidence and authenticity:** Regardless of your social standing or group affiliation, genuine confidence and an authentic personality remain powerful attractors. Focus on self-improvement, develop your strengths, and embrace your unique qualities.
- **Seeking meaningful connections:** While popularity and status can initially draw us in, true connection blossoms from compatibility and shared values. Seek individuals who resonate with your inner world and enrich your life beyond the superficial trappings of social currency.
- **Expanding your social horizons:** Stepping outside your comfort zone and interacting with diverse groups can open doors to new connections and challenge pre-existing biases. Explore different interests, engage in community activities, and broaden your social circle.
- **Remember, beauty is subjective:** Social perceptions of attractiveness are constantly evolving and vary across cultures. Embrace your own unique beauty and celebrate the diverse tapestry of human attraction.

Diminishing Attraction: When Social Factors Cast a Shadow:

While social factors can enhance attraction, they can also inadvertently diminish our interest in others. Be mindful of these potential pitfalls:

- **Obsessing over status:** Putting undue emphasis on social status can create a superficial environment where genuine connection suffers. Value individuals for their intrinsic qualities and the richness they bring to your life, not for their position on the social ladder.

- **Blindly following in-group bias:** Limiting your connections solely to individuals from your own group can restrict your personal growth and miss out on valuable perspectives. Embrace diversity, engage in open dialogues, and learn from those different from yourself.

- **Mistaking popularity for compatibility:** While popularity can be initially alluring, don't mistake it for a foundation for a lasting relationship. Seek individuals who share your values, intellectual curiosity, and life goals, as these provide a more solid ground for long-term compatibility and happiness.

Beyond the Labels: The Heartbeats of True Connection:

Ultimately, the beauty of human attraction lies in its inherent complexity and defiance of rigid categorization. Social factors like popularity, status, and group affiliation might play a role in the initial spark, but they are not the sole arbiters of lasting connection. As research by Reis and Patrick (1996) emphasizes, intimacy, attachment, and shared life experiences form the bedrock of truly fulfilling relationships.

Focus on cultivating these emotional threads with those who resonate with you on a deeper level. Practice active listening, share your vulnerabilities, celebrate each other's triumphs, and offer unwavering support during challenges. These are the cornerstones of genuine connection, the invisible threads that bind hearts together regardless of superficial social markers.

Embrace the Dance of Attraction:

The journey of attraction is a dynamic dance, where social factors, personal preferences, and emotional resonance intertwine in a captivating choreography. Learn to appreciate the diverse influences that shape your own attractions and those of others. Avoid getting blinded by superficial allure, and remain open to the possibility of connection with individuals who might not tick all the boxes on a social scorecard.

Remember, the most meaningful and enduring relationships are often forged in the quiet corners of shared laughter, heartfelt conversations, and unspoken understanding. So, step onto the dance floor of attraction with an open heart, a curious mind, and a readiness to be surprised by the beauty of genuine connection that transcends social labels and societal expectations.

A Final Note: Celebrate Your Uniqueness:

In the midst of exploring the social influences on attraction, it's crucial to remember your own unique value. Your individual personality, your passions, and your quirks contribute to the vibrant tapestry of human attraction. Don't try to conform to prescribed notions of desirability; instead, embrace your authenticity and radiate confidence in your own skin. The person who is truly attracted to you will appreciate you for who you are, social factors and all.

By navigating the intricacies of social influence without losing sight of your own intrinsic beauty and emotional connections, you can cultivate meaningful relationships that enrich your life and fill your heart with joy. Let your dance of attraction be a symphony of self-acceptance, genuine connection, and the intoxicating mystery of who you are drawn to and why.

Chapter 5. A Tapestry of Desires: How Culture Paints the Portrait of Attraction

While universal tendencies might play a role in human attraction, its true canvas is painted with vibrant cultural brushstrokes. From the idealized features deemed beautiful to the unspoken rules of courtship, cultural norms and expectations significantly shape how we perceive attractiveness and who we're drawn to.

Let's embark on a fascinating journey across continents and traditions, exploring how cultural variations weave a tapestry of diverse mating preferences.

Body Language of Beauty:

Cultures around the globe paint contrasting portraits of physical attractiveness. In Western societies, toned bodies, symmetrical features, and light skin are often perceived as ideal, reflecting historical influences and media portrayals. However, in some African cultures, fuller figures are associated with fertility and health, while elongated necks in certain Southeast Asian groups symbolize beauty and social status.

These variations extend beyond outward appearances. In India, large, expressive eyes hold significant allure, while in Japan, pale lips and smooth skin hold sway. Even hair, a seemingly universal adornment, carries cultural significance. In certain Polynesian cultures, thick, dark hair is prized, while shaved heads in Buddhist communities signify spirituality and detachment.

The Allure of Adornment:

Cultural norms extend beyond physical features, dictating the language of attraction through dress, makeup, and adornments. In cultures with strict gender roles, clothing emphasizes differences, with women adopting vibrant colors and elaborate accessories, while men adhere to more subdued styles. Conversely, in societies with greater gender fluidity, fashion choices might prioritize self-expression over rigidly defined norms.

Ritualistic adornments and modifications also play a role. Tattoos in Maori culture denote social status and ancestral connections, while nose rings in India signify marital status and wealth. Body modifications like lip stretching in certain African tribes or neck elongation in Thailand serve as cultural markers and symbols of beauty.

The Dance of Courtship:

Cultural norms extend to the intricate choreography of courtship and dating rituals. In Western societies, direct eye contact and open displays of affection are common, while in many Asian cultures, subtle gestures and indirect communication reign supreme. In some communities, arranged marriages based on compatibility determined by family and social standing remain the norm, while others embrace individual choice and romantic freedom.

Even seemingly mundane aspects of daily life carry cultural weight in the realm of attraction. In Japan, exchanging business cards follows a specific protocol, and skillful use of chopsticks can be seen as a sign of refinement and potential partnership material. Likewise, in Arab cultures, offering tea or sharing meals denotes hospitality and interest.

Beyond the Surface: Values and Traits:

Cultures not only dictate physical preferences but also shape what we find attractive in terms of personality and values. In individualistic societies, independence and assertiveness might be prized, while collectivist cultures might value conformity and family loyalty.

Religious beliefs and moral codes also play a role. In cultures with strong religious traditions, piety and adherence to spiritual values might be central to finding a suitable partner. Similarly, communities with emphasis on community service and social responsibility might seek individuals who share their commitment to the collective good.

Navigating the Crossroads:

Understanding the diverse influences of culture on attraction empowers us to navigate its intricate intersections. Here are some key takeaways:

- **Recognize diversity:** Appreciate the beauty and validity of different cultural perspectives on what constitutes attractiveness. Avoid ethnocentrism and challenge your own biases.
- **Seek genuine connection:** While cultural norms might provide initial filters, remember that meaningful relationships thrive on shared values, mutual respect, and genuine connection beyond superficial ideals.
- **Embrace open communication:** Discuss expectations and cultural differences openly with potential partners. This communication fosters understanding and helps navigate potential challenges.
- **Celebrate individuality:** Don't try to conform to cultural expectations if they don't align with your own values and sense of self. Be confident in your uniqueness and seek partners who appreciate you for who you are.

Beyond Borders: The Allure of the Mosaic:

In a world increasingly interconnected, cultural boundaries are blurring, and attraction patterns are evolving. Intercultural relationships present both challenges and opportunities. They require navigating differences in communication styles, traditions, and family expectations. However, they also bring a richness of perspective, a deeper understanding of different worldviews, and the potential for a truly unique and fulfilling connection.

A Global Tapestry of Attraction:

From the sun-kissed beaches of Rio, where toned bodies and samba rhythms ignite passion, to the serene temples of Kyoto, where quiet gestures and shared tea ceremonies whisper unspoken desires, human attraction unfolds in a dazzling global tapestry. Each culture paints its own portrait of beauty, weaving threads of physical ideals, societal expectations, and cherished values into a captivating canvas of mating preferences.

By appreciating the intricate dance of cultural influences, we can move beyond superficial stereotypes and open ourselves to the boundless possibilities of connection.

Remember, the most powerful attractor is not the perfect adherence to cultural norms, but the genuine spark of shared values, mutual respect, and the willingness to embrace the beautiful mosaic of cultural differences.

So, as you journey through the labyrinth of attraction, let curiosity be your compass, respect be your torch, and an open heart be your guide. You might just discover that the most captivating relationships blossom not within the confines of single cultural ideals, but in the vibrant kaleidoscope of shared experiences and a deep appreciation for the diverse tapestry of human desires.

A Final Note: Celebrate Your Cultural Compass:

While exploring the influence of culture on attraction, it's crucial to celebrate your own cultural heritage and its unique contribution to your identity. Your customs, traditions, and values shape your perception of beauty, your communication style, and your expectations for relationships. Embrace the richness of your cultural compass and recognize how it adds a distinctive hue to the vibrant canvas of human attraction.

By understanding the influence of culture on attraction, we can navigate the delicate dance of interpersonal connection with greater awareness and empathy. We can celebrate diversity, challenge stereotypes, and open ourselves to the boundless possibilities of love and connection that transcend cultural borders and societal expectations.

Remember, the beauty of attraction lies not in conforming to a single ideal, but in embracing the rich tapestry of human desires and the joy of forging meaningful relationships beyond the boundaries of cultural norms.

Chapter 6. The Dance of Genes: Unveiling the Evolutionary Roots of Attraction

Beyond fluttering hearts and stolen glances, the captivating symphony of attraction lies in the echoes of ancient evolutionary forces. Natural selection, with its ruthless calculus of survival and reproduction, has sculpted our preferences, shaping the traits we find alluring in potential mates. Let's embark on a captivating journey through evolutionary theory, uncovering the hidden code within our desires and exploring how the pursuit of attractiveness directly impacts our reproductive success.

The Good Genes Hypothesis:

At the heart of evolutionary perspectives on attraction lies the "good genes hypothesis," proposed by Amotz Zahavi (1975). It posits, that individuals favor physical and behavioral traits that signal genetic quality and health, ultimately enhancing the survival chances of their offspring. These "honest signals" of good genes can manifest in various ways:

- **Physical Symmetry:** Studies by Grammer and Thornhill (1994) suggest symmetrical features are perceived as indicators of good developmental stability and resistance to parasites, making them attractive qualities.
- **Healthy Appearance:** Clear skin, bright eyes, and youthful attributes may signal a strong immune system and reproductive potential, increasing their appeal.
- **Confidence and Social Status:** Research by Fink et al. (2006) found confident individuals, often associated with higher social status, are perceived as more attractive, potentially due to their

access to resources and ability to protect offspring.

Beyond the Surface: Intelligence and Personality:

Evolutionary perspectives extend beyond physical beauty, encompassing cognitive abilities and personality traits. Intelligence, as evidenced by studies is often perceived as attractive, likely due to its association with problem-solving abilities and potential benefits for offspring. Similarly, research suggests conscientiousness, characterized by reliability and responsibility, is valued in potential partners due to its positive impact on family stability and resource management.

Sex Differences: Diverging Desires:

Evolutionary perspectives also acknowledge the divergence in attraction patterns between sexes due to differing reproductive strategies. Men, typically investing less time and resources in childrearing, might prioritize physical attractiveness and reproductive potential in partners. Women, on the other hand, might seek traits like stability, resourcefulness, and paternal commitment, as evidenced by research by Buss (1985).

The Mating Game: Attraction in Action:

Attraction doesn't exist in isolation; it fuels the intricate mating game, influencing partner selection and ultimately impacting reproductive success. Studies by Buss and Barnes (1986) highlight the differences in desired traits depending on relationship goals. Individuals might prioritize physical attractiveness for short-term flings, while seeking compatibility and commitment in long-term partners.

Furthermore, research by Miller (2000) underlines the role of humor in attraction. The ability to make others laugh might signal intelligence, social skills, and emotional stability, increasing one's appeal in the mating pool.

Beyond the Universal: Cultural Nuances:

While evolutionary forces might provide a broad framework for understanding attraction, cultural variations influence how these preferences manifest. Research by Brown et al. (2004) demonstrates that body size preferences shift across cultures, with some favoring slender figures and others embracing fuller physiques. Similarly, cultural norms and expectations can shape ideals of beauty and acceptable courtship behaviors.

Beyond the Genes: The Evolving Landscape:

Modern life with its emphasis on choice and technology has introduced new dynamics to the landscape of attraction. Online dating platforms offer a broader and curated pool of potential partners, potentially shifting traditional mate selection criteria. Research by Sprecher et al. (2011) suggests online daters place a high value on education and shared interests, alongside physical attractiveness.

Additionally, social media and the emphasis on self-presentation might be altering perceptions of beauty and potentially leading to unrealistic expectations about potential partners.

Navigating the Dance: From Theory to Practice:

Understanding the evolutionary underpinnings of attraction can be a valuable tool for self-awareness and informed choices. Here are some key takeaways:

- **Appreciating the Evolutionary Framework:** Recognize how natural selection has shaped our preferences and the potential benefits of seeking certain traits in partners.
- **Balancing Evolutionary Imperatives with Individual Desires:** While acknowledging the role of evolution, remember

that your personal values, experiences, and emotional needs also play a crucial role in choosing a partner.

- **Beyond the Checklist:** Don't rely solely on evolutionary criteria; prioritize genuine connection, shared values, and compatibility for a fulfilling relationship.
- **Embracing Diversity:** Appreciate the cultural and individual variations in preferences and avoid judging others based on solely evolutionary notions of attractiveness.

A Symphony of Influences:

The story of attraction is a captivating concerto, where the melody of evolutionary imperatives intertwines with the harmonies of culture, personal experiences, and individual desires to create a unique and dynamic composition. Remember, the true beauty of connection lies not in adhering to a single script dictated by our ancient ancestors, but in embracing the richness of these diverse influences and crafting a relationship that resonates with your heart and aligns with your vision for happiness.

Beyond the Mating Game: Attraction for More Than Reproduction:

While evolutionary perspectives focus on attraction in the context of mate selection and reproductive success, it's crucial to acknowledge that human attraction extends far beyond the biological imperative.

We find ourselves drawn to friends, mentors, colleagues, and artistic creators, not primarily for their genetic potential, but for their kindness, intelligence, shared passions, and the joy they bring to our lives.

This broader lens on attraction reminds us that our capacity for connection transcends the primal urges of procreation. We connect for companionship, intellectual stimulation, emotional support, and the shared pursuit of meaning and purpose. These intrinsic human needs and desires also play a vital role in shaping whom we find attractive and with whom we choose to connect.

A Final Note: Celebrate the Tapestry of Attraction:

As we delve deeper into the evolutionary roots of attraction, let us not lose sight of the intricate tapestry that this understanding weaves. It enriches our self-awareness, empowers us to make informed choices in our relationships, and allows us to appreciate the beautiful diversity of human connection.

Remember, the allure of another is not solely measured by the degree to which they tick boxes on an evolutionary checklist. It's a vibrant interplay of physical and emotional magnetism, intellectual resonance, shared values, and the sparks of joy that ignite when two souls connect on a deeper level. So, embrace the dance of attraction in all its complexity, celebrate the diversity of desires, and allow your own unique beauty to shine forth, attracting hearts and minds drawn to the melody of who you truly are.

By understanding the evolutionary whispers hidden within our desires, navigating the cultural nuances that color our preferences, and honoring the individual yearnings of our hearts, we can weave a tapestry of meaningful connections that enrich our lives, transcend fleeting physical allure, and resonate with the profound beauty of genuine human connection.

Chapter 7. Neuroscience of Attraction

I magine walking down the street and bam! Butterflies erupt in your stomach, your palms get sweaty, and a goofy grin spreads across your face. You've just spotted someone attractive, and your brain has gone into overdrive! But what's really happening behind the scenes of this hormonal rollercoaster?

Let's dive into the fascinating world of brain science and uncover the neural mechanisms powering the magic of attraction, explained in terms even a non-scientist can understand.

The Reward Center Takes Center Stage:

Imagine your brain as a bustling theater, and the "reward center," known as the ventral tegmental area (VTA), as the star performer. When you encounter someone captivating, the VTA springs into action, releasing a potent neurotransmitter called dopamine. This chemical maestro ignites feelings of pleasure, excitement, and anticipation, making you feel like you've just hit the jackpot in the lottery of love. Dopamine whispers, "Hey, this person is special! Pay attention!"

Spotlight Mania: The Prefrontal Cortex Steals the Show:

But dopamine isn't a lone wolf. The prefrontal cortex (PFC), your brain's attention director, joins the act. It shines a spotlight on the object of your desire, filtering out distractions and amplifying their every smile, laugh, and quirk. Suddenly, the world around you fades away, and the only thing that matters is that captivating individual standing before you. The PFC ensures you don't miss a single note in the symphony of their allure.

Memory Lane: The Hippocampus Joins the Party:

Ever feel like you recognize someone you find attractive on an almost instinctual level? That's the hippocampus, your brain's memory maestro, waltzing into the performance.

It scans your vast library of past experiences and pulls out any similar feelings or moments associated with attractiveness. Maybe a certain cologne reminds you of your first crush, or the way they raise their eyebrows echoes a beloved celebrity. These familiar connections add a layer of comfort and excitement to the attraction cocktail.

Butterflies Take Flight: The Amygdala's Nervous Excitement:

But wait, why are your palms sweaty and your heart racing like a hummingbird on espresso? That's the amygdala, your brain's fight-or-flight conductor, getting a bit confused. Even though you're not facing a saber-toothed tiger, the amygdala misinterprets the intense emotions triggered by dopamine and the PFC as a potential threat.

So, it releases adrenaline, the chemical that prepares you for battle. This can result in nervousness, blushing, and even awkward stumbles – your brain's way of navigating the thrilling, yet slightly perilous, waters of attraction.

Building Bridges: Mirror Neurons Empathize:

Beyond the initial fireworks, another fascinating set of cells, the mirror neurons, step onto the stage. These specialized neurons mimic the actions and emotions you observe in others, allowing you to literally "feel" what they feel.

As you interact with the object of your interest, mirroring helps you understand their perspective, fostering empathy and connection. It's like building a bridge across brains, allowing you to cross over and glimpse their inner world.

Trust Takes Root: The Insula Weighs-In:

As your interactions deepen, the insula, your brain's trust detector, joins the chorus. This area integrates information from your emotions, bodily sensations, and memories, helping you assess whether you can trust the person you're drawn to. Trust plays a crucial role in developing intimacy and vulnerability, two essential ingredients for a lasting bond. The insula acts like a wise counselor, whispering, "Do you feel safe and secure with this person?"

The Attachment Orchestra: Oxytocin and Vasopressin Enter the Scene:

If things progress even further, the attachment center, located in the hypothalamus, takes center stage. This area releases hormones like oxytocin and vasopressin, the same ones that create the blissful bond between parent and child. These chemicals foster deeper connection, feelings of security and contentment, and the desire to stay close. Imagine an orchestra of these hormones serenading your brain, painting a portrait of intimacy and affection.

Beyond the Physical: The Higher-Order Regions Take the Lead:

But attraction isn't just a physical phenomenon. As you get to know someone better, the "higher-order" regions of the brain, like the temporal lobes and the cingulate cortex, take center stage. These areas process information about shared values, intellectual compatibility, and long-term goals. If these align, the attraction deepens, transforming into a more enduring and meaningful connection. It's like the brain's orchestra evolving from a pop band to a full-fledged symphony, playing a complex and nuanced melody of connection.

A Dynamic Tapestry: Individuality Reigns

Remember, the dance of attraction is not a pre-choreographed routine. It's a vibrant tapestry woven from the threads of your unique brain, experiences, and cultural background. Your personal preferences, past relationships, and even your current emotional state all influence who you find captivating and how your brain orchestrates this attraction. There's no one-size-fits-all template, and that's the beauty of it!

Beyond the Binary: Shades of Allure:

Attributing a binary label of "attractive" or "not attractive" to someone is both reductive and inaccurate. Attraction is a nuanced and subjective experience, influenced by a multitude of factors beyond physical features. Someone who might not initially spark a physical fire could, upon closer interaction, ignite a deep connection on an intellectual or emotional level.

Conversely, someone deemed conventionally attractive might lack the qualities you value most, leaving you uninspired. Embrace the spectrum of attraction, the possibility of unexpected connections, and the richness of discovering beauty in different forms.

The Allure of the Familiar: Mere Exposure:

Research by Berscheid (1998) highlights the phenomenon of "mere exposure," where repeated contact with someone, even without positive interaction, can increase our sense of attraction.

Familiarity triggers feelings of comfort and safety, potentially paving the way for deeper connection. This explains why long-term friends or colleagues can sometimes find themselves unexpectedly drawn to each other.

Open yourself to the possibility that prolonged interaction can unveil hidden treasures of attraction.

Passion's Orchestra: Shared Interests Drive Connection:

Passion can be a powerful magnet, drawing us to individuals who share our interests and pursuits. Whether it's a love for hiking, a dedication to social justice, or a shared obsession with obscure movies, common passions create a unique bond and foster mutual understanding. Research by Hatfield and Berscheid (1985) suggests that shared activities and experiences further enhance this connection, solidifying the attraction. Embrace the power of shared passions and let them orchestrate a symphony of connection.

The Chemistry of Compatibility: Beyond Butterflies:

While initial attraction might be fueled by dopamine and adrenaline, long-term compatibility demands a different kind of chemistry. Studies highlight the role of oxytocin and vasopressin, the "love hormones," in promoting feelings of attachment and trust. A shared sense of values, similar life goals, and effective communication create the foundation for a compatible partnership, where attraction evolves into a deeper and more sustained bond. Seek the harmony of compatible values and aspirations, not just the fleeting flutter of butterflies.

The Dance of Change: Fluidity in Attraction:

Our preferences and the very nature of attraction can undergo shifts and changes over time. Life experiences, evolving priorities, and personal growth can all influence who we find appealing. What once ignited a spark might no longer hold the same power, and new qualities might emerge as desirable. Don't be afraid to embrace this fluidity as a natural part of your journey and remain open to discovering new forms of connection you might not have anticipated.

Final Note:

Let your brain be your compass as you navigate the captivating landscape of attraction. Listen to the whispers of your emotions, pay attention to the connections that resonate with your values, and celebrate the unique dance of attraction that unfolds in your own life. By appreciating the diverse spectrum of human connections and the intricate interplay of hormones, neurotransmitters, and brain activity, you can embark on a truly enriching journey of understanding yourself and others.

Remember, attraction is not a singular, pre-defined experience. It's a vibrant tapestry woven from threads of physical allure, emotional resonance, shared values, intellectual compatibility, and the magic of familiarity. Explore this tapestry with an open mind and a curious heart, embrace the diverse threads that connect you to others, and savor the beauty of every encounter, whether it ignites a fleeting spark or becomes a beacon guiding you towards a deeper and more fulfilling connection.

Bonus Tip:

Want to boost your own attractiveness? Engage in activities that naturally release dopamine and activate the reward center, like exercise, listening to music, or spending time with loved ones. A happy brain is an attractive brain, so do things that make you feel good and radiate your inner confidence!

Additional Tip:

Pay attention to how you feel around someone and the conversations you have. The brain doesn't lie!

If you feel energized, understood, and stimulated, your brain might be telling you something special is brewing. Conversely, if you feel drained, anxious, or misunderstood, it might be a signal to re-evaluate the connection. Trust your intuition and let your brain guide you on this fascinating journey of human connection!

So, remember,

The journey of attraction is a vibrant tapestry woven by your brain's intricate neural landscape. It's not just about fleeting butterflies and heart palpitations; it's about building bridges of understanding, fostering trust, and seeking compatibility on multiple levels. Embrace the complexity, appreciate the individuality, and enjoy the ever-evolving mystery of human connection. Remember, the sparks that ignite initial attraction might just transform into a radiant fire of lasting love, fueled by mutual understanding and deep emotional resonance.

Chapter 8. Beyond the Surface: Exploring the Subtle Pull of Priming and Subliminal Cues in Attraction

The world of attraction might seem like a whirlwind of butterflies and stolen glances, fueled by undeniable chemistry and immediate sparks. But beneath the surface of these overt sensations lies a hidden orchestra of subtle cues and priming effects, influencing our perceptions and judgments in ways we often don't realize. Let's delve into this fascinating realm, uncovering the power of priming and subliminal cues in shaping our attraction to others.

Priming the Canvas of Desire:

Imagine your brain as a vast canvas, and priming as the subtle brushstrokes that influence how you "paint" the world around you. When you're exposed to certain concepts, words, or even images before encountering someone, it subtly primes your brain to perceive them in a specific light. For example, research by Bargh et al. (2001) demonstrated that participants primed with words related to warmth and kindness judged the same person to be more attractive than those primed with neutral words.

This priming effect extends beyond fleeting impressions. Studies by Bodenhausen (1993) showed that exposure to subtle cues associated with desirable personality traits, such as honesty or intelligence, can significantly influence long-term perceptions of attractiveness. It's like priming your brain to subconsciously seek these qualities in others, enhancing your overall perception of them.

Subliminal Whispers: When the Unconscious Guides the Heart:

While priming influences conscious exposure, subliminal cues operate in the shadows, sending messages directly to the unconscious mind. Research by Dutton and Aron (1974) famously showcased the power of subliminal messages, placing participants on a wobbly bridge and exposing them to subliminal messages of being "in love." Compared to a control group, those exposed to these messages expressed significantly higher levels of attraction towards the bridge experimenter.

This doesn't mean subliminal messaging can magically make you fall in love with anyone. The effectiveness depends on various factors like individual differences and existing biases. However, it showcases the potential of our unconscious to be subtly swayed by fleeting, hidden cues.

Environmental Alchemy: Setting the Stage for Attraction:

The environment itself can become a powerful priming tool, subtly influencing our perceptions of attractiveness. Studies by Guéguen (2003) demonstrate that ambient lighting plays a significant role. Warm, reddish hues have been shown to enhance perceived attractiveness, while colder, bluer tones can have the opposite effect. Even subtle arrangements like the presence of flowers or the scent of coffee can subconsciously prime us for more positive interpretations of others.

Remember, these environmental cues are not magic spells; they work in conjunction with your existing preferences and expectations. However, they highlight the fascinating interplay between external stimuli and our internal judgments of attractiveness.

The Social Alchemy of Priming: Mirroring and Contagion:

Our social interactions themselves become another arena for priming and subliminal cues. Mirroring, unconsciously mimicking the mannerisms and speech patterns of another person, can create a subtle sense of connection and familiarity, potentially enhancing attraction.

Research by Lakin et al. (2003) demonstrates this, showing that people who were subtly mirrored by their interaction partner judged them to be more likable and attractive.

Furthermore, emotional contagion, the unconscious transfer of emotions between individuals, can also play a role. If you're interacting with someone who exudes positive emotions, like joy or enthusiasm, it can prime your own brain to experience these emotions, potentially leading to increased attraction. This explains why being around happy people can sometimes make us feel happier ourselves and, in turn, find them more appealing.

Beyond Manipulation: A Call for Ethical Awareness:

While understanding the power of priming and subliminal cues can be fascinating, it's crucial to approach this knowledge with ethical awareness. Manipulating these techniques to exploit or deceive others is not only unfair but also undermines the genuine nature of human connection.

Instead, focus on using this knowledge to enhance your own interpersonal interactions. Be mindful of how your environment and behavior can subtly influence others, and strive to create an atmosphere of genuine connection and mutual respect.

Cultivating Conscious Attraction: Embracing Authenticity:

Remember, true attraction thrives on authenticity and shared values. While priming and subliminal cues can influence your initial perceptions, lasting connection will be built on genuine interactions, shared experiences, and a deeper understanding of the other person. Focus on developing meaningful conversations, finding common ground, and appreciating the unique qualities that make someone special.

Ultimately, the magic of attraction lies not in manipulating external cues but in cultivating genuine connection and celebrating the beauty of being drawn to someone for who they truly are. Embrace the conscious choice to go beyond the surface, delve deeper into the tapestry of personality and shared experiences, and let your genuine connection with others paint a vibrant and authentic portrait of attraction.

Navigating the Maze: Cultural Nuances and Individual Differences:

The captivating influence of priming and subliminal cues doesn't operate in a homogenous vacuum. Cultural norms and individual differences significantly impact how these subtle whispers sway our perceptions of attractiveness. What might be considered a prime for attraction in one culture might hold little sway in another. Similarly, individual expectations, past experiences, and personal biases can act as filters, influencing how we interpret and respond to these cues.

Cultural Tapestry:

For example, research by Dion et al. (1970 highlights the impact of cultural norms on perceived attractiveness. While symmetrical features are often considered attractive across cultures, the ideal body size and skin tone can vary significantly. Similarly, certain facial expressions or behavioral cues might be interpreted differently depending on cultural context. Recognizing and respecting these cultural variations is crucial to avoid misinterpreting attraction cues and promoting genuine cross-cultural connections.

Individual Uniqueness:

Beyond cultural variations, individual differences also play a significant role in determining how priming and subliminal cues influence our attraction. Studies by Langlois and Stephan (1975) suggest that people with pre-existing biases towards certain personality traits or physical characteristics are more likely to be primed by cues associated with those attributes. Additionally, personal insecurities or past experiences can create filters that skew our interpretations of subtle signals.

Understanding these individual nuances helps us navigate the intricacies of attraction on a personal level. Be mindful of your own biases and emotional baggage, and strive to approach others with an open mind and a willingness to embrace diversity.

The Ethical Compass: Responsible Priming and Messaging:

The knowledge of priming and subliminal cues comes with immense responsibility. As we delve deeper into the science of attraction, it's crucial to remember that manipulating these techniques for personal gain or exploiting them to deceive others is not only unethical but also detrimental to authentic connections.

Instead, focus on utilizing this understanding to create an environment that fosters genuine interaction and respectful communication. Consider how your own behavior and environment might be priming others, and strive to create a space where people feel comfortable and valued for who they truly are.

Beyond the Primed Canvas: Cultivating Authenticity:

While priming and subliminal cues can spark initial interest, genuine and lasting attraction is built on a foundation of authenticity and shared values. Focus on developing meaningful conversations, actively listening to others, and seeking out connections that go beyond fleeting physical allure or manipulated cues. Celebrate the unique qualities that make individuals special, and appreciate the beauty of being drawn to someone for their genuine personality and the shared experiences that connect you.

Embracing the Dance: A Symphony of Influences:

Remember, attraction is a complex tapestry woven from various threads, including priming and subliminal cues, cultural influences, individual differences, and ultimately, the magic of authentic connection. Embrace the diversity of this tapestry, appreciate the subtle whispers that influence your perceptions, and use this knowledge to navigate the captivating landscape of human interaction with respect, empathy, and a genuine desire to connect with others on a deeper level.

By acknowledging the nuanced role of priming and subliminal cues while prioritizing authenticity, cultural awareness, and ethical responsibility, you can approach the world of attraction with a newfound understanding and appreciation for the unique and beautiful dance of connection that unfolds between individuals.

I hope this exploration of the subtle but powerful role of priming and subliminal cues in attraction has provided you with valuable insights and encouraged you to approach interpersonal interactions with an open mind, a curious heart, and a commitment to cultivating meaningful connections.

Remember, the most profound beauty of attraction lies not in manipulating external cues or succumbing to unconscious whispers, but in embracing the authenticity of being drawn to someone for who they truly are and building a genuine connection that transcends fleeting sparks and blossoms into a lasting bond.

Chapter 9. Love in the Digital Age: How Technology has Transformed the Landscape of Attraction

———

Ah, attraction! That intoxicating whirlwind of emotions, stolen glances, and fluttering hearts. But in the 21st century, this timeless experience has found itself intertwined with a powerful force: technology. From online dating apps to curated social media profiles, the digital landscape has irrevocably altered how we meet, interact with, and perceive potential partners, fundamentally reshaping the very canvas of attraction.

Swipe Right on Serendipity: Online Dating Redefines the Game:

Gone are the days of chance encounters at the local cafe or awkward introductions through friends. Tinder, Bumble, Hinge – these modern-day matchmakers have transformed dating into a game of curated profiles, swipes, and algorithms. Potential partners are now presented as neatly packaged options, their attractiveness filtered through carefully chosen photos and witty bios.

This efficiency comes with trade-offs. While online platforms broaden our pool of potential connections, they also narrow our initial focus to superficial factors. Physical appearance often takes center stage, potentially eclipsing deeper qualities like shared values or intellectual compatibility. The constant parade of profiles can also lead to a sense of disposability, encouraging users to quickly swipe left on someone deemed "not good enough," overlooking deeper connections that might take time to bloom.

Curated Perfection: Social Media Paints a Filtered Picture:

Beyond finding dates, social media has become a potent tool for crafting our desired image, influencing how we attract potential partners. Carefully curated posts, envy-inducing travel photos, and perfectly staged group gatherings paint a picture of an idealized life, often far removed from reality.

This constant barrage of curated perfection can distort our perception of attractiveness, leading to unrealistic expectations and feelings of inadequacy. It can also create a pressure to perform – to constantly present our best selves online, potentially masking our true personalities and hindering genuine connection.

Algorithmic Alchemy: Matching Beyond the Surface:

However, technology's role in attraction isn't purely superficial. Dating algorithms are constantly evolving, aiming to go beyond physical attributes and match individuals based on shared interests, values, and personality traits. While these algorithms are far from perfect, they offer a glimmer of hope for building deeper connections based on compatibility.

Imagine finding someone who loves hiking as much as you do, shares your passion for obscure movies, or even possesses the same quirky sense of humor. Technology, albeit through imperfect means, can potentially guide us towards finding people who resonate with us on a deeper level.

The Paradox of Choice: Abundance Can Be Overwhelming:

The sheer abundance of potential partners offered by technology can be both a blessing and a curse. While having numerous options provides exciting possibilities, it can also lead to decision fatigue and paralysis of choice. This "paradox of choice" can make it difficult to commit to any one person, as the constant temptation of "what if" lingers. Furthermore, the fear of missing out (FOMO) can fuel a never-ending pursuit of the next best thing, hindering the development of meaningful relationships.

Beyond the Screen: Technology as a Tool, Not a Master:

Despite its undeniable impact, technology is ultimately just a tool in the realm of attraction. It can facilitate encounters, present potential partners, and even offer insights into compatibility. However, the real magic happens when we step away from the screen and engage in genuine interaction. Building a lasting connection with another person requires authentic conversation, shared experiences, and a willingness to be vulnerable.

Reclaiming Authenticity: Cultivating Real Connections:

In the face of digital filters and curated profiles, cultivating authenticity is crucial. Focus on showcasing your true self, both online and offline. Share your passions, vulnerabilities, and genuine interests. Seek out conversations that go beyond the surface, and prioritize developing connections based on shared values and experiences. Remember, attraction is not just about physical beauty; it's about finding someone who resonates with you on a deeper level, someone who makes you laugh, challenges you, and enriches your life.

Mindful Navigation: Building Healthy Digital Habits:

As we navigate the digital landscape of attraction, it's important to develop healthy habits.

Be mindful of the time you spend on dating apps and social media, ensuring that these platforms complement your life, not consume it. Take breaks from the digital world, and dedicate time to real-world interactions and activities that bring you joy.

Remember, your true worth is not defined by online likes or the number of matches you have.

Embracing the Evolution: Celebrating the Dynamic Nature of Attraction:

Technology's influence on attraction is constantly evolving. New platforms emerge, algorithms change, and our own preferences shift over time. Embrace this dynamic nature, and remain open to the possibilities that technology offers. Use it as a tool to broaden your horizons, but don't let it dictate your happiness or self-worth.

Beyond the Algorithm: Human Connection at its Core:

Remember, the allure of attraction and the magic of building a fulfilling relationship lie not in the algorithms of dating apps or the curated perfection of social media profiles. At its core, attraction thrives on genuine human connection, on the messy, authentic interactions that spark shared laughter, deep conversations, and a sense of belonging.

Cultivating Empathy: Seeing Beyond the Digital Facade:

In a world obsessed with appearances and online personas, cultivating empathy becomes an essential tool for navigating attraction. Look beyond the carefully crafted image and strive to understand the person behind the screen. Listen actively, ask meaningful questions, and be open to learning about their hopes, dreams, and vulnerabilities. Remember, everyone has a story to tell, a unique tapestry woven from experiences and emotions that shape who they are.

Celebrating Imperfection: Beauty Beyond Filters:

Technology often presents an idealized version of reality, fueling unrealistic expectations and anxieties about our own imperfections. Remember, beauty encompasses more than just flawless skin and symmetrical features. True attractiveness lies in the quirks that make us unique, the imperfections that tell our story, and the confidence we exude when embracing our authentic selves. Celebrate your vulnerabilities, your passions, and your quirks – these are the very things that make you truly captivating.

Prioritizing Shared Experiences: Building Lasting Bonds:

While technology can initiate connections, it's shared experiences that solidify them. Put down your phone, step away from the screen, and engage in real-world interactions. Take a walk in the park, share a meal, discuss a book, or simply sit down and talk without distractions. Shared experiences create memories, foster understanding, and build the foundation for deeper bonds that transcend the transient allure of online profiles.

The Art of Vulnerability: Opening Up for Deeper Connection:

Attraction often goes hand-in-hand with vulnerability. To truly connect with someone, we must open ourselves up, share our fears and dreams, and allow ourselves to be seen for who we truly are. This vulnerability can be intimidating, but it's also the catalyst for deep and lasting connections. When we allow ourselves to be vulnerable, we invite others to do the same, creating a space for mutual understanding and acceptance.

Embracing the Journey: Attraction as a Process, Not a Destination:

Remember, attraction is not a one-time event or a final destination. It's a dynamic process, an evolving journey of discovery. As we get to know someone, our initial perceptions can shift, and unexpected attractions can blossom. Be open to these changes, and embrace the journey of getting to know someone on a deeper level. Allow your attraction to evolve and transform organically, fueled by shared experiences, meaningful conversations, and a genuine connection that goes beyond the digital surface.

Conclusion: A Tapestry Woven with Technology and Authenticity:

In conclusion, technology has undeniably changed the landscape of attraction. It has opened doors to new possibilities, broadened our horizons, and challenged traditional ways of meeting and interacting with potential partners. However, it's crucial to remember that technology is merely a tool. The true magic of attraction lies in the authentic connections we forge, the shared experiences we create, and the vulnerability we embrace.

As we navigate this digital age of love and relationships, let us remember to celebrate our imperfections, prioritize real-world interactions, and cultivate empathy for the stories hidden behind curated profiles. Let the sparks of attraction that ignite online be nurtured through genuine conversations, shared dreams, and the courage to be vulnerable. For in the end, it is this tapestry woven with the threads of technology and authenticity that will truly capture the essence of human connection and create lasting bonds that transcend the fleeting allure of the digital screen.

So, put down your phone, step away from the screen, and embrace the messy, beautiful, and ever-evolving realm of human connection. Remember, the most captivating beauty lies not in a perfectly filtered image but in the genuine sparkle of our authentic selves and the connections we forge in the real world.

Chapter 10. Gazing into the Crystal Ball: The Future of Attraction in a World Shaped by Technology

Ah, attraction! That eternal dance of butterflies, stolen glances, and whispered desires. From Shakespeare's sonnets to modern rom-coms, it has fueled our stories and shaped our societies. But as technology leaps forward, casting its shadow on every aspect of life, we can't help but wonder: what does the future hold for this captivating phenomenon?

Let's journey into the realm of speculation, peering through the veil of the present to explore potential trends in attraction and how they might influence our interpersonal connections.

The Rise of the Digital Matchmaker: AI-Powered Algorithms Redefining Compatibility:

Forget Tinder swipes and personality quizzes. Imagine a future where artificial intelligence (AI) becomes the ultimate matchmaker, delving into the depths of your genetic code, neurochemical pathways, and even past relationship data to identify your ideal partner. Advanced algorithms, fueled by vast datasets of human behavior and preferences, could predict compatibility with uncanny accuracy, potentially guiding us towards relationships with a statistically guaranteed chance of success.

But will such AI-powered matchmaking diminish the thrill of serendipity and the joy of discovering an unexpected connection? Will we become slaves to algorithms, sacrificing the messy beauty of human intuition for the cold calculations of machine learning? While AI algorithms might offer valuable insights, it's crucial to remember that attraction is a tapestry woven from a multitude of threads, many of which defy quantifiable analysis. The spark of laughter shared over a random cup of coffee, the deep understanding born from an impromptu adventure – these are the moments that defy algorithms and remind us of the magic of human connection.

Beyond Biology: Embracing the Spectrum of Desire:

Our understanding of attraction has traditionally leaned heavily on biology, focusing on hormones, physical features, and reproductive compatibility. But the future might paint a more nuanced picture. As societies become increasingly inclusive and diverse, our understanding of attraction will likely expand beyond traditional binary paradigms. Gender fluidity, polyamory, and various forms of non-monogamous relationships might become more widely accepted, challenging the very definition of what it means to be attracted to someone.

This evolution in our understanding will redefine the future of relationships. Imagine a world where families come in all shapes and sizes, where love finds expression in countless ways, and where attraction transcends societal norms and biological imperatives. It will require a shift in perspective, a dismantling of outdated assumptions, and an embrace of the rich tapestry of human desires and connections.

Beyond the Flesh: Virtual Intimacy and the Blurring of Lines:

Technology is already blurring the lines between the physical and the virtual. The rise of virtual reality (VR) and augmented reality (AR) could further transform the landscape of attraction. Imagine falling in love with a captivating personality crafted by artificial intelligence within a breathtakingly realistic virtual world. Could such connections be just as genuine, just as meaningful, as those formed in the physical realm?

This raises ethical and philosophical questions. Will virtual relationships supplant our need for physical interaction? Will we become enamored with digital avatars, neglecting the complexities of real-world connections? While VR and AR might offer exciting possibilities for connection and exploration, it's crucial to remember that human interaction thrives on shared experiences, physical touch, and the subtle nuances of non-verbal communication. Virtual worlds can enhance our experiences, but they should never become a substitute for the richness and complexity of real-world connections.

Designer Babies and the Pursuit of "Perfect" Attraction:

As genetic engineering advances, the very concept of attraction might face an unprecedented challenge. Imagine a future where parents can choose their children's physical and even certain personality traits. Would this give rise to a generation obsessed with "perfect" partners, engineered for maximum compatibility? Would spontaneity and the beauty of unexpected connections become relics of the past?

Such a future presents ethical and social dilemmas. Who defines "perfect" traits? Will this lead to societal divisions based on genetic engineering? While genetic engineering might offer solutions for certain medical conditions, the pursuit of "designer babies" for the sake of attraction raises profound questions about our values and the very essence of what it means to be human.

Beyond the Algorithm: Cultivating Authenticity in a Wired World:

Amidst the rise of AI, genetic engineering, and virtual realities, it's crucial to remember that the future of attraction doesn't solely lie in the hands of technology. The most vital ingredient will always be: ourselves. In a world increasingly shaped by algorithms and simulations, cultivating authenticity will be more important than ever. We must strive to connect with others on a deeper level, beyond the superficial allure of filtered profiles and engineered traits.

Remember, the essence of attraction lies not in algorithms or genetic compatibility, but in the shared laughter, the whispered secrets, the vulnerabilities laid bare. It's about finding someone who resonates with your soul, who challenges you to grow, and who makes you feel truly seen and understood for who you truly are. This requires introspection, empathy, and a willingness to embrace our own imperfections. It means stepping away from the digital facade and investing in real-world experiences, meaningful conversations, and the courage to be vulnerable.

Redefining Compatibility: Shifting Towards Shared Values and Experiences:

As technology pushes the boundaries of attraction, the definition of compatibility will likely evolve. Physical features and biological determinism might give way to shared values, intellectual stimulation, and a mutual understanding of life goals. compatibility will likely hinge on the ability to build a meaningful life together, to grow alongside each other, and to face the challenges of life hand-in-hand.

This shift will redefine the future of relationships. Imagine couples drawn together by their shared passion for environmental activism, their love for exploring hidden corners of the world, or their commitment to raising compassionate and mindful children. These shared experiences and values will form the bedrock of lasting connections, offering a deeper and more enduring form of attraction than simply physical traits or genetic predispositions.

Embracing Diversity: Celebrating the Multifaceted Nature of Attraction:

The future of attraction will hopefully be a mosaic of diversity, a celebration of different forms of love and connection. There will be room for LGBTQIA+ relationships, polyamory, non-traditional families, and countless other expressions of human desire. This inclusivity will challenge outdated norms and broaden our understanding of what it means to be attracted to someone.

This inclusive future will require tolerance, acceptance, and a willingness to learn from each other's experiences. By celebrating diversity, we enrich the tapestry of human connection and open ourselves up to a wider range of meaningful relationships that defy arbitrary societal labels and embrace the true richness of human emotions.

The Dance of Technology and Humanity: Finding Balance in a Connected World:

Technology will undoubtedly play a significant role in the future of attraction. AI algorithms might offer valuable insights, genetic engineering might present new possibilities, and virtual realities might open doors to exciting experiences. However, it's crucial to remember that technology is a tool, not a master. The power to choose, to connect, and to experience genuine attraction lies within us.

The future of attraction lies in finding a balance between the possibilities offered by technology and the enduring power of human connection. We must leverage technology to expand our horizons, enrich our experiences, and connect with others on a deeper level. But we must also safeguard our authenticity, cultivate empathy, and prioritize real-world interactions that nourish our souls and foster genuine relationships.

Gazing Beyond the Horizon: A Future Filled with Possibility:

The future of attraction is a vast and uncharted territory, filled with both potential and perils. It's a landscape where AI algorithms mingle with ancient desires, where virtual romances intertwine with whispered secrets shared under starry skies. This future holds the promise of deeper connections, broader understanding, and a more inclusive tapestry of human love. But it also demands caution, introspection, and a commitment to preserving the essence of what it means to be truly attracted to another human being.

So, as we peer into the crystal ball of tomorrow, let us remember that the future of attraction is not etched in algorithms or engineered genes. It is shaped by our choices, our values, and our willingness to embrace the beautiful complexity of human connection. Let us build a future where attraction thrives on authenticity, inclusivity, and the enduring power of shared experiences that transcend the fleeting allure of technology. This is the future where love, in all its diverse forms, can truly blossom and flourish, painting the canvas of our lives with vibrant hues of connection, joy, and shared meaning.

Remember, the most captivating attractions are not found in the cold calculations of machines or the superficiality of digital profiles. They reside in the depths of our own humanity, in the vulnerability we share, the stories we tell, and the connections we forge in the vibrant tapestry of the real world. Let us embrace this future, not with fear and trepidation, but with open hearts and curious minds, ready to explore the breathtaking possibilities that lie ahead for the ever-evolving dance of attraction in a world shaped by technology.

Conclusion

As we reach the final note in our exploration of attraction, a symphony of knowledge resonates within us. We've delved into the intricate workings of the human brain, the whispers of evolution etched in our genes, and the cultural tapestries that frame beauty in a thousand hues. But amidst the fascinating facts and scientific revelations, a fundamental truth remains: **attraction is a profoundly human experience.**

Yes, science illuminates the dance of hormones and the allure of symmetry. Yet, it's the laughter shared over a cup of coffee, the vulnerabilities whispered under a starry sky, and the shared dreams that ignite passion that truly make a connection sing.

So, as you step back into the world, armed with the knowledge gleaned from these pages, remember this: The formula for attraction isn't a rigid equation. It's a vibrant painting where science mingles with intuition, and biology dances with the human spirit. Embrace the science, but never lose sight of the magic that resides within you – the unique spark that makes you, you.

Let this journey into the science of attraction be the beginning, not the end. Go forth with confidence, understanding your desires and the desires of others. Embrace the unexpected, nurture the connections that resonate, and allow yourself to be drawn to those who ignite the symphony within your own heart. The dance of attraction awaits, filled with possibilities and the promise of love in all its captivating forms.

And finally, a call to action: Share your own story! How has the science of attraction played a role in your life? Discuss your learnings, questions, and insights with others. Let's create a conversation, a vibrant tapestry woven from the diverse experiences of human connection. Together, we can continue to unravel the mysteries of attraction, celebrating the beautiful symphony that plays when hearts connect.

Remember, dear reader, the science of attraction is just the beginning. The rest, the magic, the love – that's up to you!

The End.

Don't miss out!

Visit the website below and you can sign up to receive emails whenever Pasindu A publishes a new book. There's no charge and no obligation.

https://books2read.com/r/B-A-BEABB-OOVYC

Connecting independent readers to independent writers.

Did you love *The Science of Attraction*? Then you should read *The Secret to a Great Sex Life*[1] by Pasindu A!

[2]

Do you want to have a great sex life? The key is communication.

The Secret to a Great Sex Life: 10 Ways of Talking to Your Partner About Sex will teach you how to talk to your partner about your sexual needs and desires in a way that is open, honest, and respectful. You will learn how to communicate your boundaries, identify and resolve any problems in your sex life, and strengthen your intimacy and connection.

This book is for anyone who wants to improve their sex life, regardless of their age, gender, or sexual orientation. It is especially helpful for couples who are struggling to communicate about sex or who are feeling frustrated with their sex life.

Here are just a few of the things you will learn in this book:

---

1. https://books2read.com/u/mgRqrK

2. https://books2read.com/u/mgRqrK

How to choose the right time and place to talk to your partner about sexHow to start with a positive and gently transition into what you'd like to changeHow to be specific and direct in your communicationHow to use "I" statements to communicate your needs in a non-judgmental wayHow to be open to feedback and listen to your partner's needs and desiresHow to set boundaries and communicate what you're not comfortable withHow to be patient and understandingHow to use humor and playfulness to make talking about sex more enjoyable

Why men and women must read this book:

Sex is an important part of many people's lives. It can be a source of pleasure, intimacy, and connection with our partners. However, sex can also be a source of anxiety, frustration, and disappointment. One of the biggest challenges that couples face is talking about sex openly and honestly.

This book will teach you how to talk to your partner about sex in a way that is open, honest, and respectful. By learning how to communicate effectively about sex, you can create a more satisfying and fulfilling sex life for both of you.

Here are some specific benefits of reading this book:

Learn how to communicate your sexual needs and desires more effectivelyImprove your communication with your partner in all areas of your relationshipStrengthen your intimacy and connectionResolve any problems in your sex lifeFeel more confident and comfortable with your sexualityHave a more satisfying and fulfilling sex life

If you want to have a great sex life, you need to be able to talk to your partner about it.

This book will teach you how to do just that.

Read more at https://healthfactsbydoctorpasindu.com/.

Also by Pasindu A

Find the Man of Your Dreams: 10 Traits of High-Value Men
Miles Apart Hearts Together: 10 Ways to Thrive in a Long Distance Relationship
Financial Planning for the Modern Couple: 10 Ways to Manage Your Finances in Today's Economy
The Disaster Preparedness Survival Guide: 10 Tips on How to Plan and Prepare for Any Emergency
The Secret to a Great Sex Life
The Science of Attraction

Watch for more at https://healthfactsbydoctorpasindu.com/.

About the Author

Pasindu A is a passionate writer, a doctor, and a relationship expert. He is the author of several ebooks on self-improvement and relationships, including the popular ebook "Find the Man of Your Dreams: 10 Traits of High-Value Men." Pasindu A is a gifted writer with a unique ability to connect with his readers and help them achieve their goals.

Follow him on Facebook and Instagram - "healthfactsbydoctorpasindu"

Read more at https://www.facebook.com/healthfactsbydoctorpasindu?mibextid=ibOpuV.